Whisper of the Dandelions

Karishma Dewan Nohwar

BookLeaf Publishing

India | USA | UK

Presentation by *BookLeaf Publishing*

Web: www.bookleafpub.com

E-mail: info@bookleafpub.com

ISBN: 9789360941758

First edition 2024

DEDICATION

I dedicate this book to my father. This collection stands as a tribute to his enduring love and the profound impact he has had in my life. Grieving his loss made me write more as a part of healing and I found peace in writing amidst the chaos of life. I feel the best way to express emotions is through a string of words that create a symphony. In whatever situation you may face there are always some words that play together and create a poetry true to oneself.

ACKNOWLEDGEMENT

I am encouraged to follow my heart and have always been supported by my husband, mom & sister. This has helped me evolve & keep moving forward in the process, allowing me to embrace new opportunities and experiences.

PREFACE

This is my first collection of poems, which I have written over the years. I've never shared my poetry before, but I'm excited to open up to a larger audience in the hope that someone will resonate with the diverse emotions that life presents.

In this collection, you'll find verses that explore themes of life, emotions, and nature. Each poem offers a glimpse into fleeting moments and timeless feelings, presented with sincerity and clarity.

Hello God, I called tonight

Hello God, I called tonight
To talk a little while,
I need a friend who'll listen
to my anxiety and trial.

You see, I can't quite make it
through the day just on my own,
I need your love to guide me
so I'll never feel alone.

I want to ask you to keep
me safe and sound,
Come and fill my life with confidence
for whatever fate I'm bound.

Give me faith, Dear God, to face
each hour through the day,
and not to worry over things
I can't change in any way.

I thank you God, for being home
and listening to my call,
for giving me such good advice
when I stumble and fall!

Your number, God, is the only one
that answers every time,
I never get a busy signal
never had to pay a dime.

Thank you, God, for listening
to my troubles and my sorrow
Good night, I'll call again tomorrow.

Whispered the Angels

Whispered the angels
"There's a party in heaven"
It's time to celebrate Colonel's seventy-seven!

Bring out the champagne & let it flow,
A seven-layered cake, a sight to behold.
Create memories divine,
In this moment, let happiness shine.

Shower rose petals & sprinkle some pixie dust.
Take him on a magical carpet ride,
Made from the sun's gold and rust!

Sing his favourite song,
He might not have heard since long.
Make him know that he is truly loved,
Bless his soul like a free dove.

Moments

In moments of truth
echoes the past,
Happiness and sorrow
both fleeting and vast.

Amidst waves of uncertainty
we must steer
Letting go of yesterday
facing tomorrow without fear.

With each step forward
And courage in our heart,
Smiling through uncertainty
while playing our part

In the quiet whispers of each moment
we see the truth of now
setting our spirits free
As we embrace the journey somehow!

I lit a candle for you

I lit a candle for you in my heart,
I prayed for your happiness.
Remembering the times we shared
We laughed, we cried and we cared.

Not knowing where you are,
Hoping for answers every hour
I lit a candle for you in my heart.

I look to the stars up in the sky
Knowing that you haven't given up
you're just shy!

I lit a candle for you in my heart
Praying for a new start.

I know the time was not right
Emotions held up and tight,
Even though we are far apart
You fill my life chapters' every part.

I lit a candle for you in my heart.

Her Journey

They asked her, 'Are you okay?'
With her head held high
She smiled and said, 'Never been better'
Not a twitch nor a sigh!

As they walked past her
She let her head down,
Only to realise her stole got wetter.

She pulled herself up,
Gathered the strength to stand,
Only hoping if she could get a helping hand.

She took each step in her stride,
As the pain grew stronger, she thought,
'It's a journey and I'm on a ride.'

They asked her again, 'Are you okay?'
She said with a smile,
'Thank you for asking ...
I'm trying!'

The dawn of a new day

For ever and ever I held you in my heart
Only for you to tear it apart

It took me time
lots of tears and glasses of wine,
Life seemed to have halted and pain refused to
cease.
Yet with courage, I embraced the strength to
release.

Turning you into memories, painful but with
peace.
Lessons learned, though bitter, now pave my
way
For in letting you go, I found the dawn of a new
day!

A dream

In the stillness of the earth, a dream did unfold,
Where silence reigned and stories untold.

Birds sang louder, and worms did flee,
Dogs howled mournfully, a mind not as free.

A sturdy shoulder, burdens to uphold,
Grasping right from wrong, stories untold.
Love and hate, a delicate line,
Possibilities abundant, yet left behind.

In echoes of dreams, the world stood still,
Till earth awakes, breaking silent will.

Then came the truth, a startling gleam,
Living that dream, or so it would seem.

When I see the light!

When I see the light,
I will look up at God and tell him to embrace
me.

When I see the light,
I will tell him to hold me tight and gently lead
me.

I will look upon you hoping I had a moment to
say goodbye,
So I can wipe the tear off your eye.

I would be walking on soft rose petals,
Flowers falling from heaven greeting me with
love,
I will be in peace, flying like a free dove!

A gold beam will guide me out of the darkness,
Towards the light's warmth and kindness.

I pray to be always remembered with a smile,
We made those memories that took us miles.

I will ask God to keep me with you for a while,
Till you get strong and realise that nothing went
wrong.

The day you will understand that I had to go,
I will have to move on,
And pray to God for you to carry on.

Silence in the loudest noise

I can hear the silence louder than people's
words.
I can hear the silence of the souls.
I can hear the silence as the moment passes by.
A silence within the clock ticking.
It's all silent and it's all quiet.
I can hear the silence in the loudest noise!

Life's Path

Heart whispers the words with care,
Mind composes melodies that are so rare,
While the soul orchestrates the scene
They are tranquil and serene.

The earth is our stage, where trees stand tall.
With nature's decorations, embracing all.

Winds as our audience, howling loud.
The sky, a canvas, where birds paint proud.

Be the star of your movie, in a tale you adore.
With cheers and hoots, a crowd to explore.

Life's path unfolds with the choices you take
Craft your own stage, your story awake.
Call forth your audience, the ones you hold dear.
For destiny's path, you alone steer.

Embrace the journey

In moments of weakness, find strength within.
Lost, but forging a path to begin.

When guidance seems absent, it's all around.
Open your heart, let miracles abound.

When the world feels heavy, burdens weigh.
Courage rises, leading the way!

Amidst confusion, clarity's call.
Embrace the journey, surrender all!

Truth always unfolds

There is a stillness in movement
A confusion in clarity
Peace in chaos
Monotony in variety.

Life is never what it seems,
There is always something behind the scenes.
Life's facades be told,
For the truth always unfolds.

Just Play Your Part

When you feel weak, find your might
If you are Lost, maybe your path is right.

If there is no guidance, don't you despair
Everyone is on their journey, just unaware.

Open your heart, let miracles start
They unfold when you play your part.

A Tear roll down my eye

I just had a tear roll down my eye,
When memories of you flashed by.

Made me realise that's all I have
That's the only bond that we share
What's happened is done ... And Here I am.

I just had a tear roll down my eye,
A glance through the memory lane,
Chapters unfold with our stories in pain.
Try to capture some moments, but all in vain
I just had a tear roll down my eye

Never easy to say goodbye!

That was the day, the flowers bloomed bigger,
Winds blew faster and the sun shone brighter.

The day when the angels prepared themselves to
greet you,
To take you in their arms as your pain became
lighter.

It's never easy to say goodbye!
We treasure the love you showed,
Remembering the comfort you gave to the
family you owned.

Your name was not just a name but a feeling we
held,
As you brought 'Sparkle' to our life with every
minute that went by.

It's never easy to say goodbye!
You will remain in our hearts and prayers
As the little puppy who melted our hearts.

Who made us laugh and made us cry
It's never easy to say goodbye!

That moment was mine

Unspoken words,
Unspoken dreams.
A flying dove with hopes to redeem.

Take a deep breath,
Soak in the sun, feel the grass,
Moments to take and prepare the wreath.

With the sky clearer than thoughts,
And the air fresher than a dewdrop,
Gathering memories that were brought.

Beyond time's bounds, where dreams take flight.
A ray of hope, shining bright,
For that moment was mine, in the quiet light.

It's time to be on my own

Don't cry for me,
I'm where I'm meant to be.

No need for tears
I'm happy here, with no fears.

I knew it was time to say goodbyes,
My heart is filled with sorrow
As I realize we share no tomorrow.

But I know I have to go.
As it's time to be on my own
Our journey together now ends here
Grateful to be part of your story, sincere.

You have a journey ahead, so long
Keep me in your happy song.

If a butterfly flutters near
It's my love, always with you my dear!

If the first raindrop falls,
It's me hugging through it all!

Little Girl

That little Girl loved to dance,
Give her a puddle and she'll take her chance.

Splashing through murky waters,
She believed she could never falter.

She always admired the unique shapes of the
stars,
She would love to gaze at them for hours.

She would jump to her favourite beat,
No matter if it rained or in the middle of the
summer heat.

Little by little she learnt to face obstacles,
She started viewing them with life's spectacles.

She'd giggle at her own jokes,
While some took it as a poke.

In each of us, a girl sleeps tight,
Waiting to rise with morning light.

Friendships

When the heart aches,
They are there with a balm,
Just to keep you calm!

When tears fall,
You know you can just call!

When celebrations abound,
You know your close ones are around.

There may be moments you feel
you lost your friend.
Just to find some
friendships never end!

In good times and bad you need your close ones.
We may not share the same bloodline,
But at least I know you are still mine.

Our vows

22

We take our vows for never to be apart,
Celebrating with our cherished ones,
We take the oath of taking on our part.

You and me forever and ever,
Oh so close that feeling feels my dear!

Life seems a little scary and confusing,
Your antics never stop me feeling amusing.

The laughter and cries we share,
We are our own perfect pair!

A blend of families,
All seems peculiar,
For all the craziness we share is all so familiar!

A Sailor's Journey!

A sailor steers the wheel on high and low tide,
Navigating across the oceans he goes on a ride.

Where the ocean shows no mercy,
With a brave heart he has to bow down to her
might,
Be the brightest day or the darkest night!

As the stars line up the clear sky,
The sailor burns the midnight oil.
Steering through the ocean's mystery,
As he journeys through the watery tapestry.

From one destination to another,
A sailor becomes a perfect gatherer!

From gathering memories of the mighty sea,
To playful dolphins swimming along the waves.
Oh, what a sight to see!

With a wish to return home soon with all his
adventures,
His heart set sail for shores where love still
ventures!